WORLD MYTHOLOGIES

MYTHS OF THE ANCIENT ROMANS

Pliny O'Brian

Cavendish Square
New York

Published in 2016 by Cavendish Square Publishing, LLC
243 5th Avenue, Suite 136, New York, NY 10016

First Edition

Website: cavendishsq.com

CPSIA Compliance Information: Batch #CW16CSQ

Library of Congress Cataloging-in-Publication Data

O'Brian, Pliny.
Myths of the ancient Romans / Pliny O'Brian.
pages cm. — (World mythologies)
Includes bibliographical references and index.
ISBN 978-1-5026-0994-6 (hardcover) ISBN 978-1-5026-0995-3 (ebook)
1. Mythology, Roman—Juvenile literature. I. Title.
BL803.O25 2016
292.1'3—dc23
2015032394

Editorial Director: David McNamara
Editor: Amy Hayes
Copy Editor: Rebecca Rohan
Art Director: Jeffrey Talbot
Designer: Joseph Macri
Senior Production Manager: Jennifer Ryder-Talbot
Production Editor: Renni Johnson
Photo Research: J8 Media

Abxyz/Shutterstock.com, cover; Zde/File:Zeus or Poseidon bronze 460 BC, NAMA X 15161102617.jpg/Wikimedia Commons, 4; Leemage/UIG via Getty Images, 7; DEA / G. DAGLI ORTI/Getty Images, 8-9, 10, 20, 23; PHAS/UIG via Getty Images), 13; Public Domain/File:Altes Museum - Reiterrelief Giustiniani.jpg/Wikimedia Commons; 17; Ullstein Bild via Getty Images, 26-27; DeAgostini/Getty Images, 28; Look and Learn/Bridgeman Images, 33, 41, 48, 72; Public Domain/LACMA/File:Dido and Aeneas LACMA M.81.199.jpg/Wikimedia Commons, 36; Sacchi, Andrea/Musee des Beaux-Arts, Caen, France/Bridgeman Images, 38; Sergio Anelli/Electa/Mondadori Portfolio via Getty Images, 45; Private Collection/Ken Welsh/Bridgeman Images, 52; DeAgostini/Getty Images, 59, 79; De Agostini Picture Library/Bridgeman Images, 63; Ivy Close Images/Alamy, 69; Sites Photos Alamy, 77; J. Paul Getty Museum, Los Angeles, USA/Bridgeman Images, 81.

Printed in the United States of America

TABLE OF CONTENTS

INTRODUCTION

The Importance of Mythology

A bronze statue of Zeus, king of the Greek gods, dates from about 460 BCE.

From folk heroes to gods, campfires to cathedrals, **myths** are stories that are told over and over again. These important stories deepen the identity and customs of a culture. Myths shaped the lives of the people who heard them. These timeless tales of a civilization's gods and heroes were a part of the beliefs, values, and practices of people who lived long ago.

What makes a story a myth? Unlike a narrative written by a particular author, a myth is a traditional story that has been handed down from generation to generation, first orally and later in written form. Nearly all myths tell the deeds of gods, goddesses, and other divine beings. These age-old tales were once widely accepted as true and sacred. Their primary purpose was to explain the mysteries of life and the origins of a society's customs, institutions, and religious rituals.

Mythology, the whole collection of myths belonging to a society, played an important role in ancient cultures. In very early times, people created myths to explain the awe-inspiring, uncontrollable forces of nature, such as thunder, lightning, darkness, drought, and death. Even after philosophers and scientists began to develop more rational explanations for these mysteries, myths continued to provide comforting answers to the many questions that could never be fully resolved. People of all cultures have asked the same basic questions about the world around them, such as how did the world begin, what is the purpose of living, and what happens after death?

The myths of ancient Rome are full of heroes, battles, and sacrifice. There is honor, villainy, and bravery. These myths were not just created out of people's imaginations. A civilization's geography, government, and culture all influence what stories are told, and which stories eventually become myth. For example, many of Rome's tales focus on fighting wars because Romans had to protect themselves against invasions from their many neighbors.

Mythology serves as instruction, inspiration, and entertainment. Well-known stories offer people in a society a way to express their fundamental beliefs and values and communicate these beliefs to future generations. Myths preserve and embellish tales of a civilization's accomplishments and teach important lessons about conduct and priorities. These captivating stories provided enjoyment to countless listeners and readers in ancient times, just as they do today.

The gods Castor and Pollux, twin brothers, led the Romans to victory.

WORLD MYTHOLOGIES

MYTHS OF THE ANCIENT ROMANS

PART 1: Who Were the Ancient Romans?

The Boot and the Tiber River

The Tiber River, shown in this seventeenth-century oil painting, was deep enough for navigation.

People say that Italy is formed in the shape of a boot. The peninsula juts out into the Mediterranean Sea. However, Italy is riddled with mountain ranges. At the top of the boot, before jutting out into coastline, the beautiful Alps cut off Italy from the rest of mainland Europe. Then another mountain chain, the Apennines, runs down the "boot" of Italy like a zipper. There is a narrow and dry coastal plain to the east of this "zipper." On the other side, to the west, the mountains slope down. Beyond them are the broad, fertile plains of Latium and Campania and a hilly region, which was known in ancient times as Etruria.

Nearly three thousand years ago, the ancestors of the ancient Romans settled in Latium. Their small farming villages overlooked the swift-flowing Tiber River. The Tiber was one of the few waterways in Italy deep enough for navigation. **Silt** deposited by the waters combined with volcanic ash to make the region's soil rich and fertile. Seven low hills provided dry land for homes and offered some protection from invaders. The site also offered easy access to the Mediterranean Sea. In time the hill settlements in this ideal location would grow into the mighty city of Rome.

When modern-day historians speak of the ancient Romans, they might mean the early settlers beside the Tiber River or the later citizens of Rome. They also might be referring to millions of people in hundreds of other cities across Italy, the rest of Europe, and parts of Asia and Africa. These were the subjects of the Roman Empire, one of the largest and most powerful empires the world has ever known.

Many of the most famous myths of Roman culture are set among the hills and valleys of the Latium region. The stories are often semi-historical. "The Twins of Roman Myth" on page 41, follows the mythical twins who founded the first settlement beside the Tiber River. Other tales continue the tradition by focusing on wars and leaders who shaped the history of Rome.

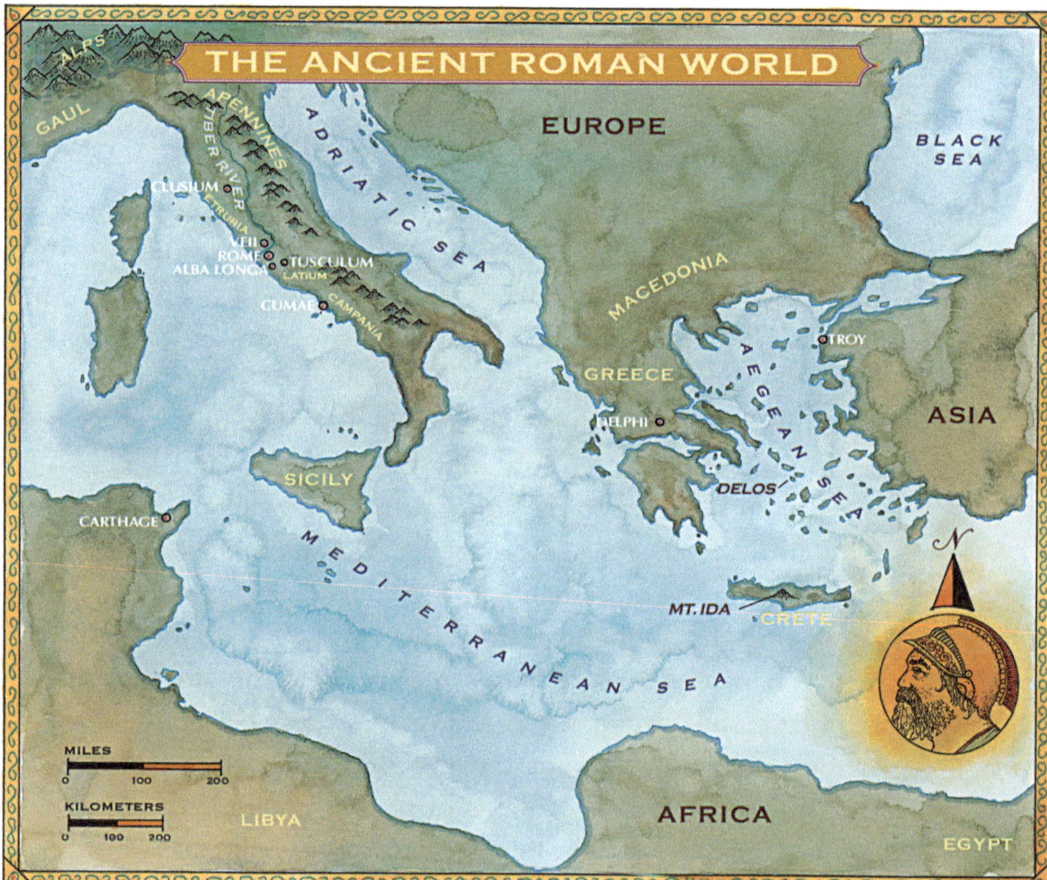

PART 1: Who Were the Ancient Romans?

From Seven Hilltops to an Empire

Augustus was the first emperor of Rome.

There are many ways of examining history, but most experts believe that the history of ancient Rome can be divided into three periods. These three periods are: the Age of Kings, the Roman Republic, and the Roman Empire.

First Period: The Age of Kings (traditionally dated from 753 to around 510 BCE)

The founders of what would become Rome were known as the **Latins**, for their homeland in the Latium region. **Archaeologists** exploring the seven hilltops of Rome have uncovered traces of Latin settlements dating back as early as 1000 BCE. Over time, these separate villages joined together to form a small city.

The city of Rome was modeled on the **city-states** of the **Etruscans** (the people of ancient Etruria in northwest Italy). Through contacts with the ancient Greeks and other cultures, the Etruscans had developed a highly advanced civilization. The Romans eagerly copied their neighbors' accomplishments. They adopted the Etruscans' alphabet, many of their artistic and religious ideas, and technical advances such as irrigation. Rome also imitated the Etruscan form of government, which was based on the rule of powerful kings.

In the sixth century BCE, Rome came under the control of Etruscan kings. Although the city made great advances during this period, the Romans resented their "foreign" rulers. Eventually, they rebelled. The kings were expelled, and the Roman Republic was born.

Second Period: The Roman Republic (traditionally dated from around 510 to 27 BCE)

The republic of Rome was governed by the Senate, several citizen assemblies, and two **consuls**. The Senate had the most power. Its decrees shaped foreign policy, public finances, and religious practices. The assemblies passed laws and elected magistrates (top government officials). The supreme magistrates were the consuls. Elected to one-year terms, these officials shared the day-to-day tasks of running the government.

Under its republican governments, Rome developed into a major power. Through a combination of war and diplomacy, the Romans gradually united all of Italy under their rule. The people of the subject territories were usually permitted to keep their own governments and way of life. In return, they had to swear allegiance to Rome, pay tribute in the form of money or goods, and provide troops to the Roman army. During the third and second centuries BCE, that mighty army defeated the great North African city-state of Carthage in a series of conflicts known as the Punic Wars. The Romans also conquered Macedonia in northern Greece, as well as kingdoms to the east and west that had once been part of the far-flung Greek empire. By the end of the first century BCE, the Roman Republic ruled over the entire Mediterranean world.

Third Period: The Roman Empire (27 BCE to 476 CE)

As Rome flexed its muscles abroad, political struggles and social unrest were stirring up civil wars at home. In 31 BCE, an ambitious young politician named Octavian ended the wars by defeating his rivals and becoming sole ruler of Rome. Four years later, the Senate gave Octavian a new name: Augustus, or "Revered One." Augustus was granted power over all of Rome's government, military, and religious affairs, making him the first emperor of Rome. During the age of Augustus, Rome entered a long period of peace and prosperity. Art, architecture, and literature flourished. Roman culture spread throughout the Mediterranean world, mingling with the beliefs and traditions of many different peoples.

Augustus was only the beginning of a long line of successful **dictators**. Rome's rule was expanded to the edges of the known world by the emperors who followed Augustus. At least sixty-five million people across Europe and including parts of Asia and Africa were living under Roman law by the second century CE.

However, this expansion could not last. Distant lands became harder and harder to control, slipping through Roman fingers. Around 285 CE, the Roman Empire was split into eastern and western halves, each with its own emperor. The western half remained Roman, while the eastern half developed into the Byzantine Empire. Finally, in 476 CE, the Roman Empire gasped its last breaths as foreign invaders conquered the remaining western half. The last emperor of Rome had been overthrown.

Social Structure in the Roman Empire

Ancient Romans on horseback are shown on this relief from about 170 CE.

Roman society was very stratified. The rich were very rich, while the poor were very poor. In the early period of the Roman Empire, the upper class was made up of a small group of rich and powerful nobles, sometimes called patricians. These patricians passed on their wealth father to son, father to son, for generations.

Eventually, during the Roman Republic, the patrician class developed into two classes, or orders. These were the senatorial class, or senatores, and the equestrian class, or equites. All men who wished to serve in the Senate had to belong to the prestigious senatorial class. However, wealthy Romans could enroll their sons in the equestrian class. These equites had the opportunity for social advancement. Equites who distinguished themselves in war or public service could rise to become senatores.

The lower class included all other Roman citizens. Any free man born to a citizen was considered a citizen himself. Lower-class citizens were called plebeians (plih-BEE-unz), or commoners. Originally, the plebeians had few rights in the patrician-controlled government. Under the republic, they gained the right to serve in the government and participate in political life through the assemblies. However, the votes of well-to-do commoners counted more than the votes of the poor.

A system known as clientship developed to protect the rights of ordinary citizens. A plebeian agreed to support a wealthy patron's political career. In return, the patron protected his client's interests, represented him in court, and helped him financially in times of need.

Slavery was an ever-present part of life in ancient Rome. Even a poor citizen might own at least one slave, while wealthy nobles often owned hundreds or even thousands. Most slaves were foreigners who had been captured in war. Depending on their talents and education, they might work as laborers, household servants, craftspeople, clerks, doctors, or teachers.

Slaves who worked hard and saved their money could eventually buy their freedom. Former slaves were called freedmen. The freedmen were not entitled to the rights and honors of citizens. They were forbidden to vote, serve in the army, perform sacrifices to the gods, or take part in public games. No matter how rich and successful they might become, they were expected to show their former masters respect, gratitude, and loyalty for the rest of their lives.

Beyond the class structure, the Roman family was equally defined. It was essentially the foundation of Roman society. Like many western societies, the man was the lord and master of the family. Women had few rights. They were not allowed to vote, hold public office, or participate in political debates. A woman's primary role in life was to marry and bear children. Consequently, they spent much of the time in the home. Despite or perhaps because of this, wives and mothers often exercised considerable influence in family decisions. Some women also played important roles in political affairs, behind the scenes.

The Evolution of the Gods

A marble bust of Mars, the god of war

While many believe that the Romans "stole" the Greek gods and goddesses, this is not true. The earliest Roman gods were divine spirits known as **numina**. These spirits inhabited all sorts of things. Nearly every natural object, situation, or place had its own numen. Some spirits dwelled in natural things such as trees or rocks, while others lived in man-made spaces such as sewers or storerooms. Numina presided over all sorts of things, including fire, lightning, hunger, jealousy, the harvesting of crops, or the wailing of babies. Every man had his own guardian spirit, or genius. Every woman had a protective juno spirit. Special spirits, known as lares and penates, would represent and protect the entire family.

In very early times, the numina had names but no physical forms or personalities. That began to change as the Romans came into contact with the peoples of other cultures, especially the ancient Greeks. The Greek gods and goddesses were vibrant individuals with strong personalities. They looked and acted like humans, only on a much grander scale. Gradually, the Romans merged these dynamic **deities** with their own native spirits. Mars, a numen of farming and fighting, became identified with Ares, the Greek god of war. Jupiter, a spirit of the sky and weather, took on all the glory of Zeus, king of the Greek gods.

In time the Romans also adopted deities from other ancient cultures, including the Egyptians and Persians. The Egyptian goddess Isis and the Persian god Mithra became important members of Rome's ever-expanding divine family. In addition, the Romans continued to worship many native gods for which the Greeks had no equivalent. These included Terminus, the Roman god of boundaries, and Janus, the two-faced god of doorways, gates, beginnings, and endings.

An endless series of religious festivals crammed the Roman calendar, happy celebrations and sober reasons for piety. Families had small altars in their homes where they made offerings to their household gods. In temples, priests performed precise rituals to honor the gods. All these celebrations and offerings were designed to appease the powerful deities who ruled the lives of the people of Rome.

PART 1: Who Were the Ancient Romans?

A Borrowing and Invention

Jupiter and Juno were king and queen of the gods.

While the numina were vitally important to early Roman society, not much was said about each numen's personality. The early Romans were more interested in the functions of a numen. A numen was supposed to be respected, but unlike most other ancient peoples, Romans did not embellish their gods. As such, Romans did not develop stories about their gods' origins, families, and histories.

However, as Rome expanded and Romans absorbed the gods of other cultures, this changed. Rome adopted the myths associated with the deities of the countries they came in contact with, often letting conquered nations keep their culture. Soon, Romans audiences were delighted by the mythological writings of the ancient Greeks and other peoples. At the same time, Roman writers and artists reimagined the "borrowed" stories in wonderful new poems, plays, paintings, sculptures, mosaics, and other works of literature and art.

The Romans did develop their own body of original stories, but these imaginative tales were not mainly about the gods. Instead, the traditional stories of Rome revolved around the origins and early development of the Roman people and their city. In many ways, these "myths" are more like **legends**, because they deal with the adventures of mortal or semidivine heroes and heroines, with the gods making only occasional appearances. In other ways, the stories fit the definition of myths. They provide a supernatural explanation for the origins of Rome's customs and institutions. They also express the high ideals and values that were an essential part of Roman civilization, such as courage, patriotism, duty, and justice. To the ancient Romans, these part-myth, part-legend stories proved that they were the most noble and virtuous people in the world. By the days of the empire, the ancient tales were also seen as proof that the gods had chosen Rome to rule all other lands.

The stories that follow are drawn from the "historical myths" or "heroic legends" of Rome. To discover the myths they borrowed of gods and goddesses, take a look through *World Mythologies: Myths of the Ancient Greeks.* Many of the Greek gods are similar to Roman ones. These famous tales have a few different retellings, but beyond details and changing the names of the gods, the tales are preserved. However, this volume contains the tales of heroes and heroines, rulers and villains.

The ROMAN GODS

The ancient Romans worshipped many of the same gods and goddesses as the ancient Greeks, but under different names. Here are some of the most important Roman deities, with their Latin (Roman) and Greek names.

ROMAN		GREEK
APOLLO	God of light, poetry, music, and science	APOLLO
CERES	Goddess of agriculture	DEMETER
CUPID	God of love	EROS
DIANA	Goddess of nature and hunting	ARTEMIS
JANUS*	God of doorways, gates, beginnings, and endings	
JUNO	Queen of the gods; goddess of women and marriage	HERA
JUPITER	King of the gods; god of light and the sky	ZEUS
MARS	God of war	ARES
MERCURY	Winged messenger of the gods; god of trade	HERMES
MINERVA	Goddess of wisdom, science, the arts, and war	ATHENA
NEPTUNE	God of the sea	POSEIDON
PLUTO	God of the underworld	HADES
SOL	God of the sun	HELIOS
TERMINUS*	God of boundaries	
VENUS	Goddess of love and beauty	APHRODITE
VESTA	Goddess of the hearth	HESTIA
VULCAN	God of fire and craftsmanship	HEPHAESTUS

* Purely Roman god

WORLD MYTHOLOGIES

MYTHS OF THE ANCIENT ROMANS

PART 2: Stories and Myths

Aeneas the Trojan, Father of Rome

An oil painting from 1598 depicts Aeneas and Anchises escaping from Troy.

The origin of a society is often steeped in myth. The early Latin people had many different stories about their origins. As time wore on, a tale of a hero named Aeneas increased in popularity and eventually became the "official" history of the founding of the Roman race.

Aeneas was one of the heroes of the famous Greek myth of the Trojan War. According to that ancient tale, he was the only member of the royal family of Troy who escaped after a Greek army captured the city. Some versions of the story say that Aeneas journeyed to Italy after fleeing Troy. The hero settled in the region of Latium, where he became the forefather of the Roman people.

The Romans were thrilled by the dramatic story of the Trojan War and were eager to claim a place for themselves in the Greeks' heroic past. Many Roman writers retold the adventures of Aeneas in stirring histories, poems, and plays. The most famous account is the *Aeneid* by Virgil. Virgil was a Roman poet who lived through the chaotic period of civil wars at the end of the republic. He wrote his **epic** poem to celebrate the new age of peace and stability established by Rome's first emperor, Augustus. The *Aeneid* confirmed the Roman people's belief that the gods had chosen their young empire to rule the world. It also held up high ideals for the Romans to follow. Throughout his travels, Aeneas demonstrates his courage and devotion to his family, his country, and the gods. In one of the most moving episodes, the hero must abandon the woman he loves, Queen Dido, in order to obey the gods' commands and fulfill his destiny.

The *Aeneid* is an enormous work sprawled over twelve books. Our retelling focuses on two highlights from Aeneas's long journey: his escape from Troy and his tragic romance with Dido.

Dramatis Personae

Dramatis Personae is a Latin phrase meaning "persons of the drama," or cast of characters. Here are the gods who play a role in the creation story of Greece:

Aeneas (ih-NEE-us) Trojan hero who founded the Roman race

Hector (HEK-tor) Former commander of the Trojan forces

Venus (VEE-nus) Goddess of love and beauty; immortal mother of Aeneas

Neptune (NEP-toon) God of the sea

Juno (JOON-oh) Queen of the gods; goddess of women and marriage

Anchises (an-KIE-seez) Prince of Troy; mortal father of Aeneas

Ascanius (as-KAY-nee-us) Son of Aeneas

Creusa (kree-OO-suh) First wife of Aeneas

Dido (DIE-doe) Queen of Carthage

Jupiter (JEW-pi-tur) King of the gods

Mercury (MER-cur-ee) Winged messenger of the gods

Lavinia (la-VIN-ee-ya) Aeneas's second wife; mother of the Roman race

Defeat at Troy

What a nightmare! Aeneas awoke with his teeth chattering and tears pouring down his face. He had dreamed that he saw his cousin Hector standing before him. In his vision, Troy's greatest champion had worn a mantle of blood and dust, just as he had on that terrible day a Greek spear took his life. "Troy is falling!" Hector's ghost had cried. "Escape before it is too late! Take the gods from their shrines and find them a new home across the seas."

> What tongue can tell the slaughter of that night? What eyes can weep the sorrows and affright?
>
> ~ Virgil, the *Aeneid*

Rising from his bed, Aeneas peered out the window. The night sky was ablaze with an unnatural light. Shouts and trumpet calls filtered through the trees surrounding his father's house. Hector's ghost had spoken true! After ten long years of **siege**, the Greeks had somehow found a way inside the city gates. Blood was spilling in the streets, and Troy was burning like a field afire when the wild winds are blowing.

Aeneas grabbed his sword and dashed out into the flames. He had no plan of battle, only rage and a fierce hunger for revenge. Quickly, the hero gathered a small band of warriors around him. Together, the men fought their way toward the royal palace. Bodies littered the streets and temple steps. Women and children ran screaming. Greek soldiers were prowling the city like hungry wolves, cutting down the innocent and slaughtering the few brave men who attempted resistance.

At last, Aeneas reached the palace. He watched helplessly as the Greeks smashed in the doors and murdered the noble old king. Suddenly, he was seized with a wild horror. He remembered his own dear father, forsaken at home. He pictured his wife and his little son, abandoned to the enemy. Glancing back to judge the strength of the forces he commanded, he saw that all his companions had died or deserted him.

At that moment, Aeneas longed for nothing more than a glorious death in battle. Just as he prepared to rush the enemy, his immortal mother, Venus, appeared before him. "Go home, my son," said the radiant goddess. "Your family awaits you under my protection. The gods themselves have conspired to destroy Troy, and no mortal hand can stop them." Then Venus lifted the veil before Aeneas's mortal vision. He saw mighty Neptune shattering the walls of Troy with his **trident**. He saw Juno lending courage and strength to the Greek forces, as she led them with sword flashing. At the sight of the dreadful powers arrayed against the city, Aeneas abandoned all hope. Turning his back on the palace, he let his mother guide him. With her help he passed safely through the flames and foes to the house of his father, Anchises.

At first, Anchises refused to leave the dying city. But when the old man saw that his devoted son was ready to die rather than desert him, he relented. With trembling hands, Anchises took the household gods from the family's altar. Gently, Aeneas lifted his aged father onto his back. The hero grasped the hand of his little son, Ascanius. He told his faithful wife, Creusa, to follow closely. Then out they went into the night of crackling flames and pitiless swords.

A wooden Trojan horse acted as a hiding place for Greeks to sneak into the city of Troy.

Slowly, the family crept through the city. They kept to the shadows, starting at the slightest noise. They had nearly reached the gates when they heard the sound of trampling feet behind them. Anchises peered into the darkness. "Make haste, my son!" he cried. "I can see the shining armor of the enemy!"

With a desperate burst of speed, Aeneas took flight, dragging little Ascanius beside him. The family raced down winding streets and dark, twisting alleys. At last, they escaped their pursuers and staggered through the gates of Troy. Gasping for air, they paused to rest at a deserted shrine outside the city. Aeneas turned to smile at Creusa and saw to his horror that she was missing.

The hero nearly went mad with grief. Hiding his father and son in a sheltered valley, he took up his weapons and headed back into danger. Silently, he crept through the burning city. He passed the bodies of the slain, the long lines of shackled captives, and the Greeks gloating over their stolen treasures. He retraced his steps all the way to his father's house, only to find it engulfed in flames.

Aeneas raised his face to the heavens and cried out his wife's name. At last Creusa answered. But the figure that appeared through the shades of night was his wife no longer. Larger than life, paler than pale, the ghost of Creusa spoke to her husband: "Do not grieve, my much-loved lord. What has happened is part of the divine plan. It is my fate to remain in Troy forever. For you, the gods have decreed hard labors and long wanderings. After many years, you shall be cast on a distant shore and found a new kingdom. With the help of the gods, you shall find a new queen and restore the Trojans to greatness."

Three times, Aeneas tried to embrace his wife. Three times, she melted away like a dream at sunrise. Finally, the hero brushed away his tears and returned to his family. To his surprise, he saw that a number of other survivors had joined them. Men and women, young and old, the wretched band of Trojans placed themselves under his command. Wherever Aeneas led, they would follow.

The morning star was rising above the crest of Mount Ida. The Greeks held every entrance to the ruined city. No hope of rescue remained. Yielding to fate, Aeneas said farewell to Troy and led his people into exile.

The Tragic Love of Dido

Under Aeneas's leadership, the Trojans built a small fleet of ships and sailed off in search of a new home. In time, they came to the island of Delos, where an **oracle** told them to seek the land of their ancestors. They traveled on to Crete, the ancestral home of one of Troy's first kings. But when they reached Crete, Aeneas's household gods appeared to him in a vision. The gods revealed that the true motherland of the Trojans was far to the west in Italy.

Their hopes renewed, the exiles set out once again. They faced many dangers and sorrows on their long westward journey. They battled the Harpies, hideous winged creatures that were part bird, part woman. They were pursued by a giant, one-eyed **Cyclops**. On the island of Sicily, so near the promised shores of Italy, Aeneas suffered his greatest loss. There the hero's father died, worn out from their long wanderings.

> From the mountain-tops, with hideous cry,
> And clatt'ring wings, the hungry Harpies fly.
>
> ~ Virgil, the *Aeneid*

As it happened, the end of their journey was not as near as it seemed. Juno had pursued the exiles ever since they had left Troy. The goddess hated the Trojans because they were fated to found a mighty kingdom that would one day conquer her favorite city, Carthage. Now she decided to destroy them once and for all. Summoning the keeper of the winds, Juno sent a violent storm. Some of the ships

After Queen Dido lost her husband, she promised to never marry again. But she found short-lived happiness with Aeneas.

sank in the mountainous waves. Others were driven onto hidden rocks and torn apart. The seven surviving ships managed to find safe harbor on the shores of Libya, in northern Africa.

Not far from the coast was the city of Carthage. The Carthaginians were a warlike people ruled by the brave and beautiful Queen Dido. After the death of her beloved husband, Dido had vowed never to marry again. But what are mortal plans compared to the will of the gods? Venus had decided that the best way to protect her son was to make the powerful queen fall in love with him. Under the goddess's influence, Dido prepared a feast for the shipwrecked Trojans. She asked their handsome leader to tell the story of their travels. By the time the hero concluded his tale, the queen was so stricken with love that all she could think of were Aeneas's looks, his words, and his valor.

Over the following days, Dido wandered about Carthage like a wounded deer with an arrow working its way to the heart. She offered sacrifices at every altar, especially those dedicated to Juno, who watches over marriage. She led Aeneas on long tours of the city, hoping to entice him with its lofty walls and strong towers. At the evening feasts, she begged the hero to tell his adventures over and over again. After they parted, she sat alone in the banquet hall, sighing with love and desire.

When Juno looked down from the heavens and saw the lovesick queen, she was struck with an idea. If Aeneas remained with Dido, he could not found the great kingdom destined to overthrow Carthage. So one day, when the queen and the Trojan hero were out hunting, Juno sent a sudden downpour. The couple took shelter in a cave. There Dido confessed her love, and Aeneas responded. The skies above flashed with fire to signal the gods' approval of their union.

For one brief season, the lovers dwelt together in perfect happiness. But their joy was not to last. The Carthaginians began to grumble that Dido was neglecting her royal duties. Their complaints reached the ears of Jupiter. The king of gods sent the winged messenger Mercury to Carthage with a stern message for Aeneas: "Worthless man! How long will you waste your days in idle luxury? It is time to remember your destiny! Will you deny your son his heritage and your descendants their fame and glory?"

The god's message left Aeneas shivering with fear and awe. From that moment, he vowed to forsake all else in obedience to Jupiter's command. Quickly, he summoned his captains. He ordered them to secretly prepare the men and ships for departure. Meanwhile, he would try to find the right words to break the news to Dido.

Dido used the sword left behind by Aeneas and killed herself.

But no arts can blind a jealous lover's eyes. Dido quickly discovered Aeneas's secret preparations and flew into a rage. "I took you in, a shipwrecked beggar, and gave you a kingdom," she screamed. "For the love of you, I sacrificed my honor. For you, I earned the contempt of my own people." Then the proud queen collapsed in tears. "If you leave me, I will die. If you ever loved me, even a little, take pity and delay your departure."

Aeneas's heart was torn by his love and pity for Dido. Still, he remembered Jupiter's message and struggled to master his agony. "Your Majesty," he said sternly, "I am in your debt for all your acts of kindness. If I had only my own happiness to consider, I would remain. But the gods have commanded me to make Italy my home, and I must obey them."

Shaken to his depths, Aeneas returned to his men. Shouting commands, he urged them to hasten their preparations. Soon, the fleet was ready to sail. With his own sword, Aeneas cut the cables. The oars churned the foam, and the ships swept across the surface of the sea.

From her watchtower, Dido saw the sails catch the winds. She tore her golden hair and cried out to the spirits of vengeance: "May the traitor who abandons me find war and suffering in Italy. May my own people oppose the race of Romans forever." Then the wretched queen took up a sword left behind by Aeneas and plunged it into her breast.

That night Carthage glowed with the flames from Dido's funeral pyre. Far out at sea, the Trojans looked back and wondered. Only Aeneas, who knew the bitter agonies of love denied, understood the message of the mounting blaze.

Even though Aeneas pressed on from Carthage, it would be a long time before his party would find their new home. They would face seven years of travel from the fall of Troy to the day they finally reached the coast of Italy. Once they reached Italy, even more troubles began. In fulfillment of Dido's curse, the tribes of Italy would declare war on the invading Trojans. The war was bloody, and did not end until Aeneas killed the Italians' greatest warrior in single combat. After that, in surrender and acceptance of Aeneas' skill in combat, the king of Latium presented his daughter Lavinia to the Trojan hero in marriage. Through their union, the blood of the Trojans and Latins would mingle and become the start of the Roman Empire.

Aeneas in the Elysian Fields

The ancient Romans believed that the souls of the dead lived on, in an underworld kingdom ruled by the god Pluto. When Aeneas reached Italy, he paid a visit to that mysterious realm. The hero entered a gloomy cave and passed the horrible creatures that guarded the entrance to Pluto's realm. He traveled on to the Elysian Fields, where the spirits of those who had lived righteous lives dwelt in happiness. There he met the spirit of his dead father, Anchises. In this passage from the *Aeneid*, Anchises shows his son a vision of the future glories of Rome.

He [Anchises], when Aeneas on the plain appears,
Meets him with open arms, and falling tears:
"Welcome (he said), the gods' undoubted race!
O long expected, to my dear embrace! ...
Long has my soul desired this time and place,
To set before your sight your glorious race;
That this presaging [foretelling] joy may fire your mind
To seek the shores by destiny designed. ...
Auspicious [fortunate] chief! thy race, in times to come,
Shall spread the conquests of imperial Rome—
Rome, whose ascending towers shall heaven invade,
Involving earth and ocean in her shade;
High as the mother of the gods in place,
And proud, like her, of an immortal race."

The Twins of Roman Myth

Twin brothers Romulus and Remus

Historians and ancient Greek writers believe that the Trojan War occurred at some point between the years 1300 to 1100 BCE. Experts in Roman history set the founding of Rome at 753 BCE. However, this leaves quite a lot of time between when Aeneas was supposed to have first arrived in Italy and when Rome was supposed to have been founded. The ancient Romans accounted for this several-hundred-year gap by coming up with a line of kings descended from Aeneas. This revised and mythological history of kings ended with one of the most popular myths of Rome, the story of Romulus and Remus.

According to Roman histories, Ascanius founded the principal city of the Latium region, Alba Longa. For three hundred years, Alban kings ruled over Latium in peace. Then a king named Numitor was overthrown by his ambitious brother, Amulius. Amulius gave orders for Numitor's newborn grandsons, Romulus and Remus, to be drowned. The babies were miraculously saved by a wolf. When they grew up, they decided to found a settlement beside the Tiber River. In a quarrel over who should rule the new city, Romulus killed his brother. He went on to found the city by himself, naming it Rome.

The myth of Romulus and Remus includes elements from Etruscan, Greek, and Roman stories dating back as early as the fourth century BCE. Near the beginning of the Roman Empire, Livy wrote what became accepted as the "true" version. Livy was a Roman historian who devoted his life to writing a 142-volume work known as *A History of Rome*. His mythological history affirmed the Roman people's belief in their natural superiority and their destiny as rulers of the world. In his account of Romulus and Remus, Livy gave this explanation for the miraculous rescue of the young princes: "The fates were resolved, I believe, upon the founding of this great city and the beginning of the mightiest of empires, next after that of heaven."

Dramatis Personae

Ascanius (as-KAY-nee-us) Son of Aeneas; founder of Alba Longa

Aeneas (ih-NEE-us) Trojan hero who founded the Roman race

Numitor (NOO-mih-tor) Rightful king of Alba Longa

Amulius (ay-MYOO-lee-us) Brother of Numitor

Rhea Silvia (REE-uh SIL-vee-uh) Daughter of Numitor; mother of Romulus and Remus

Vesta (VESTA) Goddess of the hearth

Mars (MARZ) God of war

Romulus (RAHM-yuh-lus) Founder of Rome

Remus (REE-mus) Twin brother of Romulus

Faustulus (FOWST-yuh-lus) Herdsman who raised Romulus and Remus

Saved by Wolves

After the exiled Trojan people arrived in Italy, Ascanius, son of Aeneas, founded the city of Alba Longa. For many years Alban kings descended from Ascanius ruled over the people of Latium in peace. Then a dispute arose between the sons of the thirteenth king. Before his death, the king had bequeathed the throne to his elder son, Numitor. The younger son, Amulius, refused to respect his father's wishes. Raising an army, he seized the throne and banished his brother to a neighboring kingdom. Adding crime to crime, Amulius slaughtered all of his brother's sons. He also forced Numitor's daughter, Rhea Silvia, to become a **vestal virgin**. As a priestess of Vesta, Rhea Silvia would be banned from bearing children who might one day threaten her uncle's reign.

Amulius's wicked schemes stood little chance against the will of the gods. It happened that Mars looked down from the heavens and fell in love with the beautiful Rhea Silvia. The maiden was helpless against the advances of the passionate god. In time, she gave birth to twin boys, Romulus and Remus. Amulius was furious. He had his niece thrown into prison. Then the cruel king gave orders for the infants to be drowned in the Tiber River.

At this time, the Tiber had overflowed its banks, so the king's servants could not get near the main channel. They placed the basket holding the infants in one of the pools formed by the floodwaters. The servants left, expecting the heavy basket to sink. Instead, it floated safely on the surface of the water. When the swollen waters receded, the basket came to rest on the shoreline.

Soon, a hungry she-wolf came hunting for her supper. Her sharp ears twitched at the sound of the wailing infants. The wolf sniffed the basket curiously. She gave the odd, hairless babies a lick. At last, her motherly instincts winning out over her hunger, she let Romulus and Remus drink their fill of her milk.

The she-wolf gives milk to Romulus and Remus.

A few days later, the keeper of the king's herds came upon the wolf's den. Faustulus was astonished to see the wild creature suckling the human infants. He knew all about the twin boys condemned by the king, and he suspected that these were the same children. But the herdsman also knew a miracle when he saw one. The gods clearly meant for Romulus and Remus to be saved, and he was not about to defy them. So as soon as the wolf left the den, Faustulus picked up the babies and took them home to raise as his own children.

A Deadly Disagreement

With Mars and Aeneas as ancestors, it was no wonder Romulus and Remus grew up strong, brave, and spirited. More than anything else, the young shepherds loved to go hunting. Sometimes, their prey was wild beasts. Other times, they raided the hideouts of local robbers and distributed the loot among their fellow shepherds.

One day, a band of robbers ambushed the two young men. Romulus fought off his attackers, but Remus was captured. The bandits took their captives before Amulius for punishment. They claimed that they had caught Remus raiding the herds of the king's brother, Numitor. Amulius barely gave the young shepherd a glance before turning him over to Numitor for punishment.

Meanwhile, Romulus hurried home to the man he thought was his father. When Faustulus heard what had happened, he knew that it was time to reveal the secret of his adopted sons' origins. Romulus listened attentively to the incredible story. His heart swelled with fury as he learned how the treacherous Amulius had overthrown his grandfather and abused his family. Resolved on revenge, the young shepherd journeyed to Numitor's estate. He arrived just in time to find the old king sitting in judgment of Remus. Numitor peered at the twin brothers. He noted their age and their noble bearing. Slowly, a suspicion of their true identity dawned on him. With a cry of joy, he embraced his grandsons. Then Numitor and the young princes hatched a plan to conquer the conqueror.

That night, Romulus and Remus stationed their gang of shepherd-warriors in a circle around the royal palace. Suddenly, Numitor rushed in, shouting that an enemy had invaded the city. Some of the king's guards raced off to defend the **citadel**. In the confusion, the shepherds attacked and killed Amulius. Then Numitor's voice rose above the tumult. Ordering the guards to lay down their arms, he revealed himself as the true king. Romulus and Remus marched through the crowd and hailed their royal grandfather. All the people shouted in approval as the rightful heir was restored to the throne.

Following their victory, Romulus and Remus decided to build a new settlement outside Alba Longa. Their great city would overlook the site on the Tiber River where they had been miraculously rescued as infants. But which of the noble young men should be ruler? The brothers decided to let the gods choose. Romulus would stand on one hilltop, while Remus took another. From their separate positions, each man would wait for a sign of the gods' favor.

It was Remus who received the first sign: six sacred vultures flying over his hilltop. Soon after, twelve vultures passed over Romulus. Each man was proclaimed king by his own followers—one because the gods had chosen him first, one because the gods had granted him the greater number.

The brothers' dispute quickly progressed from calm words to angry shouts and accusations. Finally, they separated; each resolved to build his own city. A few days later, Remus climbed to the top of the hill where his brother had plowed up ridges of earth to mark the boundaries of his city. Remus jumped back and forth over the low walls. He laughed at how easily an enemy could conquer the puny kingdom. At that, Romulus flew into a rage. He picked up a rock and struck his brother. "Any other man who leaps over my walls shall meet the same fate!" he shouted. Then Romulus dropped the rock in horror at the sight of his brother lying dead at his feet.

So it was that Romulus alone founded the city on the seven hills. As his first act, the new king staged a magnificent funeral for the brother he had slain in anger. But his pride was even greater than his sorrow, for he named the new city after himself: Rome.

After being taunted by his brother, Romulus attacks his brother, Remus, and kills him.

How the Sabine Women Were Kidnapped

Romulus established temples and a strong government in Rome. He created a safe haven for fugitives, in order to increase the population. Soon, his new city was strong enough to match any neighboring kingdom in war. But there was one thing it lacked: women to marry the young warriors and bear children who would ensure Rome's enduring greatness.

Romulus came up with a daring solution to this problem. He announced that Rome would host a marvelous festival, with athletic games to honor the gods. News of the event spread quickly. Visitors began to arrive from neighboring areas. The largest crowds came from the northern mountain villages of the **Sabines**. The Romans welcomed the Sabine men and their wives with great hospitality. They were even more hospitable to the Sabines' good-looking daughters.

> In derision of his brother Remus jumped over the new walls, whereupon Romulus slew him in a rage.
>
> ~ Livy, *A History of Rome*

At last came the day of the festival. All eyes were fixed on the exciting athletic contests. Suddenly, a commotion broke out. Roman men were darting through the crowds, carrying off all the young Sabine women! Mothers and fathers cried out in panic. They loudly protested the Romans' violation of the laws of hospitality. Their complaints went unanswered, as armed guards politely but firmly escorted the guests out of the city.

The kidnapped girls were shaking with fear and indignation. Romulus himself passed among them, speaking words of comfort. "Soften your anger," he said gently, "and bestow your hearts where fate has bestowed your persons. You shall be honored as married women. You shall share your husbands' prosperity, their citizenship, and, dearest of all, the blessings of children." The marriageable men of Rome echoed his pleas. They assured their chosen brides that they had acted out of love and admiration. The young men promised to be considerate husbands and make up for the loss of parents and country.

Soon the young women were reconciled to their fate. They married and settled down to run their households and bear children. But back home, the tears and lamentations of their parents continued. Finally, the Sabines gathered an army and attacked Rome. Through a combination of fierce fighting and trickery, they managed to capture the citadel. The next day, the Romans staged a heroic charge and recovered their ancient fortress.

> The young Sabine women [were] seized and given in marriage to the men of the best Roman families.
>
> ~ Cicero, *On the Commonwealth*

Now the two armies confronted each other on a muddy field in the heart of the city. Each side was prepared to fight to the death in the defense of honor and the hope of glory. But before the signal for battle could be sounded, the Sabine women threw themselves between the hostile forces. They begged their fathers not to make them widows. They begged their husbands not to give them the sorrow of a murdered father. "If you resent being related by marriage, take your fury out on us," the women pleaded. "Better to die than to lose either husband or parent, to be widowed or orphaned."

The thought of harming their wives and daughters finally persuaded the men on both sides. A hush fell among the men and officers. Neither wanted to end the day with blood on their hands. Then, the leaders of both sides put away their swords and negotiated an end to the fighting. The Sabines and Romans not only made peace but decided to combine their states under one government, marrying the two cultures forever.

The Traitor Tarpeia

According to traditional tales, the Sabine army entered Rome with the help of a young Roman woman. Tarpeia was the daughter of the officer in command of the Roman citadel on the Capitoline Hill. She stole her father's keys to the fortress and opened the gates to the enemy. Ancient Roman historians gave varying explanations for her actions. Some said that the girl was bribed with gold. Others maintained that the handsome Sabine king, Tatius, promised to marry Tarpeia in exchange for her help. Whatever her motives, in all of the tales, her fate was always the same. After the Sabines stormed through the gates, they heaped their shields on Tarpeia, crushing her to death.

Modern-day historians trace this story back to an ancient Etruscan goddess named Tarpeia. The goddess gave her name to the Tarpeian Rock, a steep cliff on the Capitoline Hill. During the Roman Republic, convicted murderers and traitors were thrown to their deaths from the Tarpeian Rock. The Romans may have invented the story of Tarpeia to explain that practice. The following verses by the first-century BCE Roman poet Propertius spell out the moral of the story: traitors are always despised, even by those who benefit from their actions.

The gateway sold, her city crushed by foes,
She [Tarpeia] claimed her fee: to wed [on] the day she chose.
Tatius, who though a foeman loathed her crime,
Said: "Come, my bed and throne are yours to climb."
Battered beneath his followers' shields she fell:
A bridegroom's gift that paid her service well.
The traitorous guide has given the hill its name:
False guardian, thus unjustly crowned with fame.

PART 2: Stories and Myths

The Six Kings of Rome

Numa Pompilius was the second king of Rome.

Roman history was often compromised for the sake of a good story, but these tales often dealt with the specific origins of Roman culture. One such example is the myths of the rulers who followed Romulus. The myths tell of six kings, each of whom made important contributions as rulers of Rome:

Numa Pompilius was a man of peace who introduced many religious rites and ceremonies.

Tullus Hostilius was a warrior whose conquests expanded the kingdom.

Ancus Marcius earned renown for both his military and administrative skills.

Lucius Tarquinius Priscus was an Etruscan immigrant who began several major building projects.

Servius Tullius enlarged the city and organized society according to wealth and property.

Lucius Tarquinius Superbus, also known as Tarquin the Proud, murdered Servius Tullius and seized the throne. His reign of terror led to the downfall of the monarchy.

There is probably a kernel of truth behind the stories of the six Roman kings. Early Rome was most likely ruled by kings, including some who were Etruscan. For the most part, though, the early Roman histories are a blend of traditional tales and creative writing. Roman writers invented these stories to fill in the period between the supposed founding of the city in 753 BCE and the beginnings of the Roman Republic around 510 BCE. Their imaginative histories explained the origins of government institutions, religious practices, and other aspects of Roman society. The myths also offered inspiring examples of heroism, patriotism, and other virtues valued by the Roman people. The stories of Tarquin the Proud provided a mythical explanation for the end of the monarchy, while reflecting the Romans' pride in their republican system of government.

The following tales are set in the reigns of three of the kings: Numa Pompilius, Tullus Hostilius, and Tarquin the Proud. Our retellings are based on a variety of early sources. These include writings by the ancient Greek biographer Plutarch*, the Roman historian Livy, and the Roman poet Ovid.

The Strange Sacrifices of Numa

After Romulus had ruled Rome for nearly forty years, he was raised up to join the gods in the heavens. At first, the Romans quarreled over who should fill his empty throne. Finally, the Senate granted the citizens the power to choose their own monarch. When the voting ended, the senators ratified the people's choice: the wise and virtuous Numa Pompilius.

Numa gave the warlike city of Rome a new foundation in peace. He taught the Romans to fear and honor the gods. He established priesthoods and appointed priestesses to guard the flame of Vesta. He also reformed the calendar, setting aside some days for worship, others for business. Through his good example, he inspired the people of Rome to behave properly out of devotion to the gods and respect for their oaths rather

* To learn more about Plutarch, check out *World Mythologies: Myths of the Ancient Greeks*.

Dramatis Personae

Romulus (RAHM-yuh-lus) Founder of Rome

Numa Pompilius (NOO-ma pom-PILL-ee-us) Second king of Rome

Vesta (VESTA) Goddess of the hearth

Egeria (ih-JER-ee-uh) **Nymph** married to Numa

Jupiter King of the gods

Tullus Hostilius (TULL-us hahs-TILL-ee-us) Third king of Rome

the Horatii (ho-RAY-she-eye) Triplet brothers who fought for Rome

the Curiatii (kyoo-RAY-she-eye) Triplet brothers who fought for Alba Longa

Horatius (ho-RAY-she-us) Roman hero who defeated the Curiatii

Lucius Tarquinius Superbus (LOO-shus tar-KWIE-nee-us SOO-per-bus) Last king of Rome; also known as Tarquin the Proud

Servius Tullius (SIR-vee-us TULL-ee-us) Sixth king of Rome

Sextus Tarquinius (SEX-tus tar-KWIE-nee-us) Youngest son of Tarquin the Proud

Collatinus (kah-LAH-tih-nus) Husband of Lucretia

Lucretia Virtuous wife of Collatinus

Lucius Junius Brutus (LOO-shus JOO-nee-us BROO-tus) Founder of the Roman Republic than fear of punishment. The Romans followed Numa willingly, for they knew that his wife and adviser was the nymph Egeria. Each night the king met with his divine wife in a sacred grove. There, Egeria instructed him in religious rites and approved the new laws that he proposed.

It was said that Numa's understanding of the gods was so great that he once dared to match wits with Jupiter. The king was seeking a charm to protect the people from lightning. Egeria told her husband how to summon Jupiter. The father of gods was not happy about being brought down from heaven. Numa's heart fluttered and his hair stood on end as he peered up at the angry deity towering over him. With an effort, the king regained his senses. "Father of the high gods," he said, "please accept my prayers and grant the people relief from your lightning bolts."

"You must make a sacrifice," bellowed Jupiter. "I demand the head—"

"Of an onion," Numa put in quickly.

"Of a man," continued Jupiter.

"Yes, you shall have the hair of a man," agreed the king.

"And the life of—" said the god.

"A fish!" exclaimed Numa.

At that, Jupiter burst out laughing. "Very well," he said. "From now on, these things will be a sufficient sacrifice to charm the lightning: the head of an onion, human hair, and a fish. And to you, O man who is not afraid of talking with gods, I pledge a great empire."

When the king told the people about his meeting with Jupiter, some were slow to believe him. So the next day, Numa summoned all the citizens to the palace. He prayed for a sign of the god's promise. His prayer was answered with three loud claps of thunder. Then a strangely shaped shield fluttered down from the sky.

> Three times the god thundered, and hurled his lightning.
>
> ~ Ovid, *Fasti*

The marvelous shield was the fortune of Rome, so the king took care to protect it. To fool thieves, he had eleven other shields made exactly like it. He also appointed a special priesthood to guard it. Numa's precautions kept the sacred shield safe through his long and peaceful reign. And in the years that followed, Jupiter kept his promise, making Rome a very great empire indeed.

Horatius and the Sister's Beam

After the death of Numa, the people of Rome chose Tullus Hostilius for their next king. Tullus was a man of war. Under his reign, Rome declared war on its neighbor, Alba Longa. The two armies prepared for battle. Just as the fight was about to begin, their leaders agreed on a plan to prevent unnecessary bloodshed. Each side would choose a champion. These warriors would fight each other. The outcome of their contest would determine which country remained free and which won dominion over the other.

It happened that there was a set of triplets in each army. On the Roman side were the three brothers of the noble Horatii family. On the Alban side were the three Curiatii. The two sets of brothers eagerly accepted the challenge. They would fight on behalf of their gods, their people, and the fate of their countries.

> With swords drawn, the triplets rushed to the charge as if they were complete armies.
>
> ~ Livy, *A History of Rome*

The six brave young men stepped onto the open field between the lines of battle. The signal sounded. The tiny forces rushed to the charge like mighty armies. Swords flashed. Blood flowed. Soon all three Curiatii were wounded, and two of the Horatii lay dying. The Alban army cheered, and the Romans lost all hope as the three Curiatii surrounded their sole remaining champion.

Young Horatius knew that he was no match for three challengers so he ran, not from cowardice but with the idea of separating his opponents. After a moment he looked over his shoulder. As he had hoped, the Albans were chasing him at different speeds, each according to his wounds. Turning suddenly, Horatius cut down his nearest pursuer. As the second man limped up, he killed this adversary, too. Now the contest was even. But the remaining Alban was exhausted and disheartened by the slaying of his brothers. "Two of you I have sacrificed to the spirits of my own brothers," cried Horatius. "The third I offer to the triumph of Rome over Alba Longa." With that, the young Roman plunged his sword into the throat of his opponent.

Horatius marched back to Rome at the head of the victorious army. Outside the city gates, he met his sister. She had been promised in marriage to one of the fallen

The Horatii and Curiatii brothers battled on behalf of their gods and their countries.

Curiatii. When she saw her lover's cloak thrown over her brother's shoulder, she cried out in sorrow.

"Have you no thought for your dead brothers?" shouted Horatius. "For the one who returns in triumph? For your country?" Then, in his rage, the champion stabbed his sister in the heart. "Thus may any Roman woman perish who mourns for an enemy!"

The people gasped in horror at the hero's dreadful deed. Horatius was taken before King Tullus, who condemned him to death. Because of his great service to the country, he was permitted to appeal the king's decision to the Assembly. His aged father spoke on his behalf. Weeping bitter tears, the old man begged the citizens of Rome not to leave him childless. He pointed to the Curiatii's weapons, hanging on a pillar. "A little while ago, you saw my son marching in triumph," he said. "You cheered the champion who brought you liberty. Will you now see him whipped and hanged from a tree, before the weapons of your enemy?"

The people were moved by the tears of the father and the courage of the prisoner. They voted to free Horatius. In order to make amends for his son's crime, the grateful father performed special sacrifices. Horatius himself signaled his submission by passing under a wooden beam erected across the street. The "Sister's Beam" would remain standing for many years in Rome, a reminder that not even a hero may take the law into his own hands.

The Tragedy of Lucretia

The last king of Rome was Lucius Tarquinius Superbus. Tarquin was a great general whose conquests expanded the kingdom. But this one virtue was overshadowed by his many faults. For Tarquin was a tyrant. He gained the throne by force, after murdering his father-in-law, the good king Servius Tullius. He held on to power through intimidation, exiling or executing all who opposed him. He governed solely on his own authority, without consulting the Senate or the people. For his arrogant conduct, the Romans gave their hated king a suitable name: "Tarquin the Proud."

Tarquin had three sons who were just as ruthless as their father. Worst of all was the youngest son, Sextus Tarquinius. One day, during a siege of a neighboring city, Sextus was dining with the Roman officers. Each man began to boast about the virtues of his wife. The rivalry grew heated. Finally, a young noble named Collatinus suggested a way to settle the dispute. "Let us take horse and inspect our wives' characters in person," he proposed. "There is no better proof than what a man sees when he comes home unexpectedly."

Flushed with wine, the young men eagerly agreed to the plan. They galloped off to Rome, arriving just as darkness fell. The group proceeded from one house to another, only to find their wives idling away their time at lavish dinner parties. Last of all they came to the home of Collatinus. There they found his wife, Lucretia, tending to her spinning by candlelight.

The young men congratulated Collatinus on his worthy wife. Then they headed back to camp. But one among them was already hatching a villainous plot. Enraptured by Lucretia's beauty, grace, and virtue, Sextus Tarquinius was determined to possess his friend's wife.

A few days later, Sextus returned to Collatinus's house alone. He was welcomed and shown to a guest room. That night he drew his sword and sneaked into Lucretia's bedchamber. Frightened from her sleep, the woman listened as the prince declared his love. He begged. He threatened. He promised her a kingdom. Lucretia steadfastly refused him. Finally, Sextus swore that he would heap scandal on her family by killing her and placing the body of a male slave in bed beside her. At that, the poor woman had no choice but to submit to his demands.

When morning broke, Lucretia sent an urgent summons to her father and husband. The men hurried home, accompanied by their trusted friend Lucius Junius Brutus. "Is all well?" Collatinus asked his wife.

"What can be well for a woman when she has lost her chastity?" replied Lucretia. "Sextus Tarquinius has stolen my honor. You must swear that you will not let his crime go unpunished."

With heavy hearts the men gave their word. Then they tried to console Lucretia, blaming the sin on the sinner and not his helpless victim. Despite their pleas, the pure and steadfast woman plunged a dagger into her heart.

Lucretia's husband and father were paralyzed with grief. But Brutus drew the dagger from the wound. "I swear by this blood," he said, "that I will banish Tarquin the Proud and all his accursed family. Never again will any man rule over Rome."

Brutus marched to the **Forum** with Lucretia's kinsmen. He called on the Romans to take arms against their oppressors. His words roused a people weary of tyranny and eager for freedom. Rebellion swept the land. The king was overthrown, and his sons joined him in exile.

> Brutus ... incited them to take up arms, as befitted men and Romans.
>
> ~ Livy, *A History of Rome*

PART 2: Stories and Myths

Tales of a New Republic

Lucius Junius Brutus, founder of the Roman Republic

When experts in Roman history examine the facts, is not clear how Rome transformed from a monarchy headed by kings to a republic of representatives. However, the Romans themselves considered the facts to be crystal clear. The poets and historians who looked back on the end of the age of kings considered it a heroic revolution. Poems and written histories speak of the overthrow of Tarquin the Proud around 510 BCE, which signaled Rome's liberation from tyranny.

Like the stories of the Roman kings, the traditional histories of the republic are a blend of reality and mythology. These imaginative tales tell of Rome's constant wars with its neighbors, struggles between the social classes, and conflicts among the city's leading families. The stories provided the Roman people with inspiring examples of virtuous behavior. They also served the purposes of Roman nobles. Historians who were sponsored by Rome's leading families often invented or rewrote "historical" tales to give their patrons illustrious ancestors. A family that could claim descent from a hero of the early republic gained status and political power.

Two famous heroes from the founding of the republic appear in the following tales. Lucius Junius Brutus, who played a role in our earlier story of Lucretia, was said to have been one of Rome's first consuls. Horatius Cocles was a courageous soldier who prevented an Etruscan army from overrunning the city. This Horatius was a descendant of one of the triplet brothers in the noble Horatii family. His legendary deeds were an added source of pride for Rome's Horatii family.

Dramatis Personae

Lucius Junius Brutus (LOO-shus JOO-nee-us BROO-tus) Founder of the Roman Republic

Lucius Tarquinius Superbus (LOO-shus tar-KWIE-nee-us SOO-per-bus) Last king of Rome; also known as Tarquin the Proud

Lars Porsenna King of Clusium

Publius Horatius Cocles (PUB-lee-us ho-RAY-she-us KAHK-leez) Hero who saved Rome from the Etruscans

Brutus, Bumbling Wiseman

In his youth, Lucius Junius was regarded as a simpleton. A nephew of Tarquin the Proud, he learned early to hide his intelligence so that the ruthless king would not consider him a threat to the throne. He even endured the nickname Brutus (meaning "dullard" or "stupid") without complaint. Meanwhile, under the veil of that insulting name lay the cunning mind that would free Rome from tyranny.

One day, Tarquin sent his three sons to the famous oracle of Delphi in Greece. The princes brought along their dull-witted cousin to amuse them. At the cave of the oracle, each of the Romans offered a gift. Brutus's offering was a golden rod concealed inside a hollow wooden staff, a symbol of his hidden character. The oracle accepted the gifts. Then a voice echoed from the innermost depths of the cave: "Whichever one of you shall be the first to kiss his mother shall be the next leader of Rome."

The excited princes drew lots to decide who would kiss their mother first on their return home. Brutus thought that the oracle had a different meaning. The moment the travelers reached Rome, the clever young man pretended to stumble and fall. As his royal cousins laughed, he kissed the earth, mother to all Romans.

It was not long after this adventure that Brutus revealed his true nature and led the rebellion against Tarquin and his family. Following the overthrow of the tyrants, the Romans eagerly embraced their liberty. No longer would they be ruled by a single king with unlimited powers. Instead, they established a republic in which the rule of law was more powerful than any one man. To head their new government, they elected two consuls, limited to terms of one year only. Among the first pair of consuls was the man honored as the founder of the republic, Lucius Junius Brutus.

As consul, Brutus confronted the first grave threat to Rome's newly won liberty. The danger came not from foreign enemies but from within the republic itself. Certain young nobles who had been friends of the Tarquin princes were discontented with the new government. Under the monarchy, they had been free to do whatever they pleased. Now all citizens were equal before the law. These young men grumbled among themselves about the loss of their special privileges. When envoys from the exiled king whispered in their ears, they were more than ready to listen. The traitorous Romans agreed to secretly admit the royal family into the city. After the Tarquins recovered the throne, those who had helped them would once again live like princes themselves.

Fortunately, the plot was discovered in time. The conspirators were captured and thrown into prison. Among them were several youths from Rome's leading families, including two sons of Brutus.

> The natural anguish of a father was apparent on Brutus's face as he performed his duty as public executioner.
>
> ~ Livy, *A History of Rome*

As chief magistrate of Rome, Brutus presided over the trial. All eyes were fixed on him as he pronounced judgment on his own children. With stern dignity, the father watched as his sons were tied to the stake and beaten. With anguish on his face, he saw them laid out on the ground and beheaded. Thus the consul put the good of the state above the most precious interests of self and family. For his sacrifice, it has been written that Brutus performed an even greater service to Rome than Romulus did in founding the city.

Horatius the Brave

After Tarquin the Proud failed to regain the Roman throne through treachery, he turned to open war. Tarquin was of Etruscan descent, so he appealed to the kings of the Etruscan cities for help. Two allies took up his cause, only to be defeated by the Romans. Finally, Tarquin went to Lars Porsenna, ruler of Clusium. The former king implored Porsenna not to allow a fellow Etruscan to wander as a penniless exile. He also warned Porsenna about the dangers of ignoring the new fashion of expelling monarchs. Unless kings vigorously defended their authority, all people everywhere might be tempted to demand liberty.

Tarquin's arguments were persuasive. Lars Porsenna was soon convinced that the security of his own kingdom depended on the presence of an Etruscan on the Roman throne. Accordingly, the king gathered his powerful army and marched on Rome.

> As the enemy drew near, everyone from the surrounding countryside fled into the city.
>
> ~ Livy, *A History of Rome*

As the Etruscans drew near, the Romans abandoned their farms and took refuge inside the city walls. Guards were posted in a giant protective circle around Rome. The city seemed secure behind its massive stone walls and the natural barrier of the Tiber River. But there remained one vulnerable point: a narrow wooden footbridge over the Tiber.

A soldier named Publius Horatius Cocles was stationed at the bridge on the morning the enemy attacked. The Etruscan forces rushed down on the Roman defenders like a bolt of thunder. At the sight of the onslaught, most of the guards threw down their arms and fled. Horatius tried desperately to stop them. Seizing one guard after another, he begged them not to desert their posts. "If we abandon this position, we will soon be fighting the Etruscans inside Rome itself!" he cried. "Stay and destroy the bridge. I will hold off the enemy as long as possible." Then Horatius marched to

Tarquin the Proud and his youngest son, Sextus, sought to regain Rome.

the head of the bridge and stood with his sword drawn, one brave man against an army.

His stirring example halted the mad flight. The guards picked up their swords and began hacking at the supports of the bridge. Two noble Romans, ashamed of their earlier panic, took their place at Horatius's side. Together, the three men put up a ferocious defense and beat back the enemy's first assault.

Now the timbers of the bridge were nearly cut through. Horatius ordered his two companions to save themselves. All alone, he challenged the Etruscans to attack again. "Come, you slaves of tyrants!" he called defiantly. "Come, you fools who attack the liberty of others without a thought for your own!"

The Etruscans hesitated for a moment, impressed by the warrior's reckless courage. Then the lead soldiers raised their battle cry and hurled their spears. Some of the weapons struck the hero's shield. Some found their mark on his flesh. Still Horatius held his ground, wounded but unshaken.

Suddenly there was a loud crash. The bridge collapsed into the river. Horatius was stranded on the far shore. "Father Tiber," he cried, "I beseech you to receive this soldier in safety." With that, he dove into the river. Still clad in his armor and clutching his weapons, he fought the swift current. Somehow, as the spears of the enemy rained down all around him, he made it across to safety.

As Horatius made it to Roman shores, his people greeted their champion with loud cheers. They carried Horatius into the city, singing songs of joy and victory. As a reward for his service and bravery, Horatius was given as much land as he could plow a furrow around in a single day. The Roman people also raised a bronze statue of Horatius in the center of the city. There his visage would grace the city for many years, allowing future generations to marvel at his valor and cherish his memory.

Gods of Victory

According to ancient Greek and Roman histories, Tarquin the Proud found a new ally after the defeat of Lars Porsenna. The ruler of the Latin city of Tusculum, who was married to Tarquin's daughter, went to war on behalf of the exiled king. In 499 BCE, the Romans defeated the Latin army at the Battle of Lake Regillus. Dionysius of Halicarnassus, a first-century BCE Greek historian, described how two gods, Castor and Pollux, led the Romans to victory.

> It is said that in this battle two men on horseback, far excelling in both beauty and stature those our human stock produces ... charged at the head of the Roman horse [cavalry], striking with their spears all the Latins they encountered and driving them headlong before them. And after the flight of the Latins and the capture of their camp, the battle having come to an end in the late afternoon, two youths are said to have appeared in the same manner in the Roman Forum attired in military garb, very tall and beautiful and of the same age, themselves retaining on their countenances [faces] as having come from a battle, the look of combatants, and the horses they led being all in a sweat. And when they had each of them watered their horses ... and many people stood about them and inquired if they brought any news from the camp, they related how the battle had gone and that the Romans were the victors. And it is said that after they left the Forum they were not seen again by anyone, though great search was made for them. ... The next day, [the Romans] concluded ... that it was the same gods who had appeared in both places, and were convinced that the apparitions had been those of Castor and Pollux.

PART 2: Stories and Myths

An Empire Is Built

Roman general Marcus Furius Camillus conquered Veii with Juno's help.

When the Roman Republic was in its infancy, it faced many enemies. Proactive against attack, the Romans struck out against would-be invaders. The location on the Tiber River was greatly envied, and they intended to keep it. Beginning in the fifth century BCE, they launched attacks across the Italian Peninsula. By 272 BCE, Rome was the master of Italy.

One of the first major victories in Rome's rise to power was the capture of the powerful Etruscan city of Veii (pronounced VEE-eye). According to traditional histories, Rome besieged Veii for ten years. Then a Roman general named Marcus Furius Camillus was granted the emergency powers of a dictator in order to bring the long war to a conclusion. Camillus conquered Veii with the help of the goddess Juno. After his victory, the Roman people turned against him, and he went into exile. He later returned to rescue Rome from invading tribes known as the **Gauls**.

Modern-day historians believe that there is some truth behind the story of Camillus. The Romans did conquer Veii sometime around 400 BCE. About ten years later, the Gauls captured Rome. After a brief occupation, the invaders left the city, probably after being paid a large ransom. As always, ancient Roman historians blended fact and fiction in their accounts of these events. In their writings, the war with Veii took on many of the dramatic elements of the Greek story of the Trojan War. The Gauls' invasion was explained as a punishment sent by the gods, perhaps because of the unjust exile of Camillus. Instead of falling to the invaders, the Romans held out on the Capitoline Hill. Instead of paying a shameful ransom, they were saved by the timely arrival of Camillus's army. According to Livy's *A History of Rome*, Camillus then drove out the Gauls "with steel, not with gold." Thus, one of the most humiliating episodes in Roman history was transformed into a tale of heroism, patriotism, and triumph.

Dramatis Personae

Marcus Furius Camillus (MAR-kus FYOO-ree-us ka-MILL-us) Heroic Roman military commander

Juno (JOON-oh) Queen of the gods; goddess of women and marriage

Sol God of the sun

Victory at Veii

Rome and Veii were bitter enemies. Rome sat on the right bank of the Tiber River, while the Etruscan city sat farther north on the left bank. The Romans were determined to capture their hated neighbor and gain sole control of the vital waterway. But Veii was a large city with towering walls. It could not be taken by storm. So the Romans surrounded Veii and settled in for a long siege, hoping to starve their enemies into submission.

In the autumn of the tenth year of the siege, the Romans were alarmed by a strange occurrence. A small lake to the south of Rome suddenly began to rise. It had been a scorching summer. All the other lakes and rivers had dwindled or dried up completely. Now, without any rainfall or other natural cause, Alban Lake swelled to the tops of the hills surrounding it.

It was clearly a message from the gods. When a Roman soldier captured an aged soothsayer from the besieged city, the meaning behind the message became clear. The Romans forced the captive to reveal a secret known only to the Etruscan oracles: Veii would never fall until the waters of Alban Lake were drained.

Quickly the Romans set to work digging channels from the lake. The water flowed in hundreds of small streams to the nearby fields. After a few weeks, the lake was dry. Then the people of Rome knew that the fate of Veii was sealed.

To carry out the conquest, the Senate appointed the statesman Marcus Furius Camillus as dictator. The commander enrolled fresh troops to fill out the weary army camped outside Veii. He swore to the gods that he would celebrate great games in their honor if they would grant a happy conclusion to the war. Then the dictator marched his army to the doomed city.

Outside the walls of Veii, Camillus devised a brilliant plan for entering the city. His men would dig a secret underground passage leading into the heart of the enemy's citadel. While some of the soldiers kept the enemy busy at the walls, others worked on the tunnel. Soon the dictator was able to send word to Rome that victory was in sight. At that, the Senate issued a public notice. Any citizen who wished to share in the fortunes of war should go out to the camp at Veii.

Within a few days, an enormous crowd had left Rome and swelled the army camp. Camillus ordered his soldiers to prepare for battle. He offered prayers to Juno, the protecting goddess of Veii. The dictator beseeched the goddess to leave the enemy city and follow his army home to Rome, where a new temple worthy of her majesty awaited her. Then Camillus gave a signal, and the citizens who had come into camp threw themselves at the walls of Veii.

The defenders ran to the walls, wondering why the Romans were suddenly rushing toward them like madmen. While their attention was diverted, the real danger was unfolding beneath their feet. A handpicked company of Roman soldiers was quietly filing down the tunnel beneath the walls of Veii. The shaft led directly under the temple of Juno. The soldiers could hear the king of Veii offering a sacrifice for the deliverance of the city. The words of a priest filtered through the earth: "Victory shall be granted to whoever cuts out the entrails of the beast." As soon as the soldiers heard this prophecy, they burst through the roof of the tunnel into the temple. They captured the king and the priests. Then they snatched up the innards of the sacrificial animal and carried them to Camillus, who himself performed the sacrifice.

> As the king of Veii was sacrificing … the Romans opened the tunnel [and] seized the entrails.
>
> ~ Livy, *A History of Rome*

With victory assured, some of the Roman company raced to the walls and attacked the defenders from behind. Others flung open the city gates to let in the rest of their army. The streets of

Veii echoed with the clash of arms and the shrieks of the wounded and dying. The struggle was long and furious. At last, the fighting slackened. Then Camillus proclaimed that all who laid down their arms and surrendered would be spared. That put a stop to the bloodshed.

After the fall of Veii, the Romans scattered in search of plunder. The wealth of the city far exceeded expectations. As Camillus saw his happy countrymen cart away their treasures, he raised his hands to the heavens. "Our victory today is great indeed," he prayed. "If any of the gods deem it to be too great, may they punish me instead of Rome." As the dictator finished his prayer, he stumbled and fell. Later, many would see that as a sign of his own condemnation.

This is the left part of an Italian fresco painting, showing the Triumph of Camillus.

The next day a group of young men were chosen for the honor of entering Juno's temple. The men purified their bodies and dressed all in white. They reverently lifted up the goddess's statue. The sacred image proved light and easy to transport, as though Juno were moving of her own accord. After an uneventful journey, the queen of gods took her everlasting seat in a temple atop the Capitoline Hill in Rome.

For the next four days, there was public rejoicing. On the fifth day, the dictator himself entered Rome. His triumphant return exceeded anything that had ever been seen before. Like the great god Sol himself, Camillus rode in a chariot pulled by four magnificent white horses. The people cheered the brilliant spectacle. At the same time, many felt a twinge of alarm at the sight of a mortal man placing himself on an equal footing with the gods.

A Savior from the Gauls

After his victory over Veii, Camillus resigned the office of dictator. He continued to serve as Rome's most illustrious military commander. Despite his many victories, the common people gradually came to despise him. They had been offended by his arrogant return from Veii. They were further inflamed when he insisted that they give up one-tenth of all the spoils from the conquered city as a gift to the gods. In time, the people's anger led to false accusations that Camillus had stolen a portion of the spoils for himself. The general was found guilty of the crime and ordered to pay a fine. Rather than endure so great an indignity, he resolved to go into exile.

Marcus Furius Camillus abolished the weighing of gold between the Gauls and the Romans.

With a heavy heart, Camillus left his beloved city. As he reached the gates, he lifted his face to the heavens. "With the gods as my witness, I am driven from Rome through no fault of my own," he declared. "May the people quickly repent of their malice and cry for my return."

Again, Camillus proved himself a man of destiny. Not long after he went into exile, the Gauls swept down from the north like a tide of divine vengeance. In the absence of the one citizen who could have made Rome's defeat impossible, the barbarians quickly overpowered the city's defenders. Many Roman soldiers were killed. Many others fled in panic. All of Rome was captured except the Capitoline Hill, where the supreme gods resided in their sacred temples. The last remaining defenders took refuge with their wives and children in the citadel at the top.

> A silvery goose went fluttering through a golden Colonnade, honking out an alarum, that the Gauls are on us.
>
> ~ Virgil, the *Aeneid*

One moonlit night, the enemy silently crept up the steepest side of the hill. They nearly caught the guards sleeping, but the sacred geese in Juno's temple sounded the alarm with their honking and flapping of wings. Aroused by the clatter, the Romans grabbed their weapons, and the citadel was saved.

Unable to conquer Rome by force, the Gauls laid siege to the city. After seven months, the people were brought low by hunger. Now they faced a bitter choice: starve or pay the enemy a fortune to bring the siege to

Juno, queen of the gods

an end. A peace conference was convened. The price for liberty was set at one thousand pounds in gold.

Just before the shameful transaction was completed, trumpets sounded outside the walls of Rome. Marcus Furius Camillus had arrived with an army drawn from the thousands of Roman soldiers who had fled at the start of the invasion. Camillus ordered his soldiers to take away the gold. He warned the Gauls to prepare for battle. Then, with the help of the gods and the resolve of soldiers determined to avenge their humiliating defeat, Camillus delivered his country from the hands of the enemy.

After the victory against the Gauls, the people of Rome thanked Camillus with tears of joy. The city's honor had been restored, and they did not have to face a life of subjugation. From then on, Camillus would be known as the father of his country. And for centuries more, Juno would smile down on the people of Rome from her holy temple, mother and protector of them all.

The Glories of Rome

Livy tells us that Rome lay in ruins after the attack of the Gauls. When a group of officials proposed moving the capital to Veii, Camillus gave this powerful speech urging his fellow citizens not to abandon their motherland. In the end, the Romans decided to rebuild their shattered city. The Rome that rose from the ashes would not fall again to foreign invaders until the end of the empire more than eight hundred years later.

> Has our native soil, this land we call our motherland, so slight a hold upon us? Does our love for our country cling only to its buildings? Unpleasant as it is to recall my sufferings [during exile], still more your injustice, I will nevertheless confess to you that whenever I thought of my native City all these things came into my mind—the hills, the plains, the Tiber, this landscape so familiar to me, this sky beneath which I was born and bred—and I pray that they may now move you by the affection they inspire to remain in your City, rather than that, after you have abandoned it, they should make you pine with home-sickness. Not without good reason did gods and men choose this spot as the site of a City, with its bracing hills, its commodious [large] river ... a sea near enough for all useful purposes, but not so near as to be exposed to danger from foreign fleets; a district in the very centre of Italy—in a word, a position singularly adapted by nature for the expansion of a city ... This has hitherto been your Fortune; what sense can there be—perish the thought!—in making trial of another Fortune? Even granting that your valor can pass over to another spot, certainly the good Fortune of this place cannot be transferred. Here is the Capitol. ... Here is the Fire of Vesta; here are the Shields sent down from heaven; here are all the gods, who, if you remain, will be gracious to you.

GLOSSARY

archaeologists Scientists who study the physical remains of past cultures to learn about human life and activity.

citadel A fortress protecting a city.

city-state An independent state made up of a city and its surrounding territory.

consuls The high magistrates of the Roman Republic.

Cyclops A giant with a single eye in the center of its forehead.

deities Gods, goddesses, and other divine beings.

dictator A high magistrate of the Roman Republic, who was temporarily granted supreme powers to deal with an emergency.

epic A long narrative poem celebrating the deeds of legendary or historical beings.

Etruscans The people of Etruria, an ancient region in northwest Italy.

Forum The center of Rome, where most business and political activity took place.

Gauls An ancient people whose homeland was Gaul, a region in Western Europe that included present-day France and Belgium.

Latins The people of the Latium region in west-central Italy. Latin can also refer to the language of ancient Latium and Rome, which became the dominant language of Western Europe.

legend A traditional story that may involve ordinary mortals as well as divine beings and may be partly based on real people and events.

mythology The whole body of myths belonging to a people.

myths Traditional stories about gods and other divine and sometimes mortal beings, which were developed by ancient cultures to explain the mysteries of the physical and spiritual worlds.

numina The divine spirits that inhabited every place, action, and natural object; the singular form is numen.

nymph One of the minor goddesses of nature who dwelled in the mountains, forests, and waters.

oracle A priest or priestess who conveyed the gods' words to humans.

Sabines An ancient people who lived in the Apennine Mountain region northeast of Latium.

siege A battle tactic in which an attacker surrounds a fortress or city, cutting off supplies to force the enemy to surrender.

silt Small particles of earth deposited by water.

trident A spear with three prongs.

vestal virgin A priestess of Vesta, responsible for tending the sacred fire on the goddess's altar. Vestal virgins took a vow forbidding them to marry or have children.

BIOGRAPHICAL DICTIONARY OF ROMAN WRITERS

Following are brief biographies of the ancient Roman poets and historians mentioned in this book.

Livy 59 BCE–17 CE
Full name: Titus Livius
Livy was a Roman historian who lived during the reign of the first emperor, Augustus. He wrote *A History of Rome*, a massive work that traces Roman history from the founding of the city in 753 BCE to 9 BCE. Only 35 out of the 142 volumes of this monumental text have survived. The first ten volumes include retellings of many Roman myths, including the adventures of Aeneas and the story of Romulus and Remus.

Ovid about 43 BCE–17 CE
Full name: Publius Ovidius Naso
The Roman poet Ovid belonged to a circle of writers and thinkers who flourished during the reign of Augustus. His masterpiece was the fifteen-volume epic poem *Metamorphoses*, which retells hundreds of ancient Greek and Roman myths. Ovid's other major works include the poem *Fasti*, which describes many of Rome's sacred rites and festivals, and the *Heroides*, a collection of imaginary letters from famous mythological women to their husbands and lovers.

Propertius about 50–16 BCE
Full name: Sextus Propertius
Propertius was a poet who lived during the age of Augustus. Very little is known about his life. His best-known surviving works are the *Elegies*, four books of love poems that have become an important source of information about the people, society, and mythology of ancient Rome.

Virgil 70–19 BCE
Full name: Publius Vergilius Maro
The son of a farmer, Virgil devoted his youth to studying Greek and Roman literature and poetry. Eventually his literary talents won him the patronage of Emperor Augustus. Virgil's most famous work was the epic poem the *Aeneid* (pronounced uh-NEE-id), which traces the adventures of Aeneas, mythical founder of the Roman race. Virgil began composing the *Aeneid* in 29 BCE and worked on it until he died ten years later. According to some accounts, he asked that the incomplete work be destroyed after his death, but Augustus insisted on publishing it instead.

FURTHER INFORMATION

Books

Bolton, Lesley. *The Everything Classical Mythology Book*. Avon, MA: Adams Media, 2002.

Fagles, Robert. *The Aeneid*. New York: Penguin Classics, 2008.

Freeman, Philip. Oh My Gods: *A Modern Retelling of Greek and Roman Myths*. New York: Simon & Schuster, 2013.

Hamilton, Edith. *Mythology: Timeless Tales of Gods and Heroes*. New York: Grand Central Publishing, 2011.

Hinds, Kathryn. *The Ancient Romans*. New York: Benchmark Books, 1997.

———. *Life in the Roman Empire: Religion*. New York: Benchmark Books, 2005.

López-Ruiz, Carolina. *Gods, Heroes, and Monsters: A Sourcebook of Greek, Roman, and Near Eastern Myths in Translation*. New York: Oxford University Press, 2013.

Masters, Anthony. *Roman Myths*. New York: Peter Bedrick Books, 1999.

Morales, Helen. *Classical Mythology: A Very Short Introduction*. New York, Oxford University Press, 2007.

Paige, Joy. *Roman Mythology*. New York: Rosen Publishing, 2006.

Websites

Encyclopedia Mythica: Roman Mythology

www.pantheon.org/areas/mythology/europe/roman/articles.html

This online encyclopedia contains hundreds of brief articles on the gods, goddesses, and legendary heroes of ancient Rome. .

History for Kids: Ancient Rome

www.historyforkids.org/learn/romans

History for Kids is an educational site presented by an associate professor of history at Portland State University. The section on ancient Rome includes information on a wide variety of topics, including Roman history, government, society, art, and religion. Click on "Roman Language and Literature" for further information on some of the ancient writers and texts featured in this book..

Windows to the Universe, World Mythology

www.windows2universe.org/mythology/worldmap_new.html

Created by the University of Michigan, this excellent site gives visitors a choice of information presented at beginning, intermediate, or advanced levels. Click on the word "Roman" on the world map for information and art relating to the Roman gods and heroes.

SELECTED BIBLIOGRAPHY

Allan, Tony, and Piers Vitebsky. *Triumph of the Hero: Greek and Roman Myth*. Amsterdam, Netherlands: Time-Life Books, 1998.

Barnett, Mary. *Gods and Myths of the Romans.* New York: Smithmark, 1996.

Cotterell, Arthur. *Classical Mythology*. New York: Lorenz Books, 2000.

Dupont, Florence. *Daily Life in Ancient Rome*. Translated by Christopher Woodall. Cambridge, MA: Blackwell, 1992.

Gardner, Jane F. *Roman Myths.* Austin: University of Texas Press, 1995.

Grant, Michael. *Roman Myths.* New York: Charles Scribner's Sons, 1971.

Livy. *A History of Rome: Selections*. Translated by Moses Hadas and Joe P. Poe. New York: Modern Library, 1962.

Ovid. *Metamorphoses*. Translated by David Raeburn. New York: Penguin, 2004.

Plutarch. *Plutarch's Lives: The Lives of the Noble Grecians and Romans*. Translated by John Dryden and revised by Arthur Hugh Clough. New York: Modern Library, n.d.

Rosenberg, Donna. *World Mythology: An Anthology of the Great Myths and Epics*. Lincolnwood, IL: Passport Books, 1986.

Virgil. *The Aeneid of Virgil.* Translated by John Dryden. New York: Macmillan, 1965.

QUOTATION CITATIONS

Quoted passages in sidebars come from the following sources:

"Aeneas in the Elysian Fields," page 40, from T*he Aeneid of Virgil*, translated by John Dryden (New York: Macmillan, 1965).

"The Traitor Tarpeia," page 51, from Propertius, *Elegies*, Book IV, translated by A. E. Watts, in Michael Grant, *Roman Myths* (New York: Charles Scribner's Sons, 1971).

"Gods of Victory," page 71, from *Dionysius of Halicarnassus, The Roman Antiquities*, translated by Earnest Cary, at penelope.uchicago.edu/Thayer/E/Roman/Texts/Dionysius_of_Halicarnassus/6A*.html

"The Glories of Rome," page 83, from Livy, *A History of Rome*, translated by the Reverend Canon Roberts, at mcadams.posc.mu.edu/txt/ah/Livy/Livy05.html

INDEX